Harley-Davidson Motorcycles

Jesse Young

Capstone Press

MINNEAPOLIS

Printed in the United States of America.

Capstone Press • 2440 Fernbrook Lane • Minneapolis, MN 55447

Editorial Director   John Coughlan
Managing Editor   John Martin
Copy Editor   Gil Chandler
Technical Advisors   Dan Cunningham and SJ Eldred

Library of Congress Cataloging-in-Publication Data

Young, Jesse, 1941-
    Harley-Davidson Motorcycles / Jesse Young.
       p. cm.
    Includes bibliographical references and index.
    ISBN 1-56065-224-1
    1. Harley-Davidson motorcycle--History--Juvenile
    literature. [1. Harley-Davidson motorcycle. 2.
Motorcycles.] I. Title.
    TL448.H3Y68   1995
    338.7'6292275'0973--dc20   94-26767
                                           CIP
                                          AC

ISBN: 1-56065-224-1

99 98 97 96 95   8 7 6 5 4 3 2

Table of Contents

Chapter 1

Harleys

You don't just ride a Harley from one place to another. You and the machine make a team. The motorcycle thunders down the road to your own heartbeat.

Whether you're motoring across a flat desert, or taking some sharp mountain curves, riding a Harley is powerful fun. You are not trapped inside, as you are in a car. Instead, you become part of the outdoors, and a part of your Harley.

The Harley-Davidson is more than a motorcycle. It's a work of art and a marvel of engineering. It's motorcycle history on two wheels. The Harley is a legend.

Chapter 2
Sturgis

Every year, during the hot days of August, a crowd of motorcyclists gathers in the small town of Sturgis, South Dakota. There are thousands of them–more than 100,000, in fact. They outnumber the residents of the town by about 20 to 1.

To get to Sturgis, the outsiders travel over America's back roads and interstate freeways. They come from all corners of the United States and Canada. And they all come the same way–riding on the back of a Harley-Davidson motorcycle.

One biker has been riding out to Sturgis every summer for years. He comes from Milwaukee, the home town of Harley-Davidson, Inc. He wears leather and jeans and, of course, a beard.

His name is William G. Davidson, but everybody calls him Willie G. He is the grandson of Arthur Davidson, one of the founders of Harley-Davidson. Willie G.'s job is to design motorcycles. Ever since 1963, he's been making Harleys look sleek and powerful.

Willie G. designed the FXS Low Rider as well as the XLCR Custom Racer. His studio also created the FX 1200 Super Glide, the Electra Glide, and many other world-famous models.

Willie G. has put his personal mark on the modern Harley motorcycle. But he's only a part of a long and fascinating story. This story stretches back to the early years of the 20th century. It covers nearly the entire history of motorcycling.

And, as any Harley rider will tell you, it is a story with a happy ending. There are more Harley owners and riders today than ever before. There are also more kinds of Harleys to ride than ever before. Harley-Davidson has created something unique: an American product that is the best of its kind in the world.

Chapter 3
The Harley-Davidson All-Stars

Harley-Davidson has made all kinds of motorcycles during its history. Designs of frames, engines, drive trains, and exhaust systems have changed with the times and with the needs of riders. But there are several models created over the years that stand out. These are the bikes that have made Harley-Davidson famous for its engineering, design, and workmanship. These are the Harley classics.

After first appearing in 1957, the Sportster caught on fast with riders who wanted a small, agile bike.

The Sportster

The first of the Harley "superbikes," the XL Sportster, first rolled out of the factory in 1957. The Sportser's 883-**cubic centimeter V-Twin** engine included big intake ports for high performance. It was a small and agile bike that made motorcycling fast and fun. By the 1990s, four models of Sportster were available, including a powerful 1200cc model.

The Duo Glide

   Created in 1958, this handsome machine quickly became the favorite of the California Highway Patrol. The troopers, and thousands of civilian riders, liked the whitewall tires and hydraulic suspension, which offered a smooth and comfortable ride. The Duo Glide's 74-cubic-inch engine also offered a lot of power.

The Electra Glide

With a new electric starter, the Electra Glide of the 1960s was a new kind of Harley. The redesigned aluminum **engine heads** also gave the Electra Glide more horsepower. In 1972, the company added a 10-inch disc brake on the front wheel. This made it the first factory-built motorcycle with hydraulic brakes in the front and the rear. The Electra Glide became one of the most popular bikes in the company's history, even as Japanese motorcycles began invading the U.S. market in the 1960s and 1970s.

The Super Glide

The FX-1200 Super Glide of the 1970s was meant to combine a heavy frame and a sporty front end. It had a lean profile and a comfortable, laid-back feel. Later Super Glide riders could choose between electric and kick starters. By 1990 the FX models carried 1340cc engines, and a **drive belt** had replaced the old **chain drives**.

The Low Rider carried customized parts—but it rolled off the assembly line in the thousands.

The Low Rider

This was the first of Harley-Davidson's "factory customs"–motorcycles with a **customized** look. It was a new version of the FX Super Glide with special parts and accessories. Low Rider Sports and Low Rider Convertibles later extended the line.

The Tour Glide

The FLT Tour Glide came out in the 1980s with a redesigned front frame and forks. The new design gave the bike an incredibly smooth and comfortable ride—ideal for long-distance traveling. A 1340cc **Evolution engine** was standard equipment. The company also offered special paint and trim, cruise control, an intercom system, and rear speakers on the Tour Glide Ultra Classic, which also could haul a sleek, carpeted sidecar.

Chapter 4

The Davidsons and the Harleys

The very first Harley was designed by Bill Harley and Arthur Davidson (the grandfather of William G. Davidson). Harley and Davidson were good friends and next-door neighbors. They also worked together at a Milwaukee factory. In their spare time, they drew up plans for a motorized bicycle.

Soon Walter Davidson, Arthur's brother and a skilled mechanic, joined the two friends. By 1903, the three men had produced a one-**cylinder** engine that fit into the frame of a bicycle. They produced three models that year in a workshop in the Davidsons' back yard.

Because Bill Harley designed the machine, his name came first. Harley and his partners produced eight motorcycles in 1904 and sixteen in 1905.

After building the motorized bicycle, Arthur Davidson spent most of his time convincing dealers around the United States to sell Harleys. Later he brought the Harley to the rest of the world.

In 1907, the Harley-Davidson Motor Company was **incorporated**. The company turned out 150 motorcycles. In the next year, Walter Davidson used the Harley Single to win the New York Two-Day Endurance Run, from the Catskill Mountains to New York City. That race made the Harley-Davidson motorcycle famous overnight.

Arthur and Walter's oldest brother, William, became manager of the Harley-Davidson plant in Milwaukee. William was a popular boss.

The first Harley-Davidsons added a one-cylinder engine to a bicycle frame.

Employees called him the "heart" of the company, while Walter was the "head."

The V-Twin Legend

In 1909, Harley-Davidson introduced the V-Twin engine. The two engine **cylinders** sat in the frame of the bike like the letter "V."

But almost as soon as the V-Twin hit the streets, its **intake valves** began to cause trouble.

The company withdrew the model and Bill Harley went to work on the engine. By 1911, the V-Twin was back on the road with a new engine. Harley-Davidsons still use this basic design.

The V-Twin look and its **torque**-pulling power make it a legend. This engine rumbles with a deep, vibrating sound. Some Harley riders even say that you can *feel* a Harley before you *see* it.

The V-Twin design goes all the way back to 1909. Harley-Davidson motorcycles still use it.

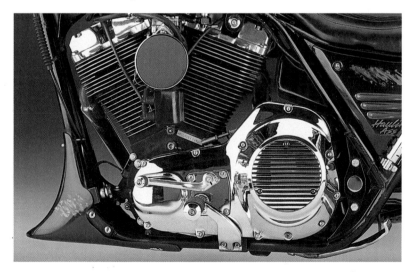

Chapter 5

Hard Times
and Hell's Angels

At times the Harley was on top. The 1920s was the "Golden Era of Motorcycles." But during the Great Depression of the 1930s, people had little money for gas and none for motorcycles. Harley-Davidson sales sank along with the economy.

The Hell's Angels did not help Harley-Davidson, either.

The Image of Hell's Angels

During World War II, members of U.S. bomber squadrons used motorcycles for

transportation in Europe. When they came home after the war, many of them felt restless. They wanted freedom from the everyday world. Riding their motorcycles helped these veterans take their minds off their problems. Some of them joined motorcycle gangs.

On July 4, 1947, a motorcycle gang called the Hell's Angels roared onto the Main Street of Hollister, California. The gang terrorized the town, or so the story goes. *Life* magazine published a photograph (discovered later to be a fake) showing the motorcyclists as **vandals**, drunks, and **rebels**.

The members of the Hell's Angels rode only Harleys. That was part of their code. But the Harley-Davidson Company did not want the Hell's Angels, or any other violent group, to be associated with the Harley name.

Then, in 1953, came a powerful movie called *The Wild One*, starring Marlon Brando. Brando rode an Indian motorcycle in the movie and his gang all rode Harleys. The movie convinced Americans that motorcycles were for rebels.

As the 1960s began, rock 'n roll and hippies began changing people's attitudes toward motorcycles. The Harley became a symbol of freedom and good times. Harley-Davidson sales increased. But the good times did not last long.

Harley Struggles to Compete

In 1965, Honda, a Japanese motorcycle company, began competing with Harley-Davidson in the United States. Their smaller models were a big success. To compete, Harley-Davidson started making lightweight bikes, but that did not help. Their old customers were not interested in lightweight motorcycles.

In 1969, American Machine Foundry (AMF) bought the Harley-Davidson company. The new owners ordered the Harley factory to build more motorcycles in a shorter time. For many years, Harley-Davidson made only low-quality, lightweight machines.

In the early 1980s, Harley-Davidson employees bought the company back from AMF. They started making heavyweight Harleys again. They also developed the new Evolution engine, also known as the Blockhead engine.

Another motorcycle boom started in 1983. This time Harley-Davidson was ready with a better motorcycle–the Super Glide. The company launched the new model in 1984 at Sturgis, South Dakota. The Super Glide was a big hit with Harley riders.

Chapter 6

Customizing A Harley

A few years back, reporters from *Motor Trend* magazine wanted to find out what the Harley magic was all about. They took three factory models–a 883 Sportster, a Low Rider Custom, and the Heritage Softail Classic–and rode the Pacific Coast Highway in California.

But when they stopped, Harley riders just laughed at them and their factory-made, stock exhausts. Along the way, the reporters counted over 500 different Harleys in different sizes, shapes, and **configurations**. The reporters learned that customizing is a big part of the Harley magic.

When Harley-Davidson marked its 90th birthday in 1993, one dealer celebrated by creating "Wide Bro." He started by welding a wider fuel tank to a 1990 Softail. He also widened the fiberglass rear fender. His customizing increased the bike's value to

$25,000. But the average person could do exactly the same thing in an ordinary garage.

With new parts and accessories, Harley riders put their personal touch on their machines.

Chapter 7
Racing

You would have to go back to ancient chariot races to get a thrill that compared to early motorcycle racing. Around 1910, as many as 25,000 people gathered to watch these spectacles.

The Harley-Davidson company always made sure that Harleys were in those early races. After all, racing was the only way to show off the power of their motorcycle. Harley-Davidson supported the American Motorcycle Association in order to keep the sport alive. As a result, the company had great influence on racing rules.

Harley's top place in these races lasted until 1961. Then the American Motorcycle Association allowed Japanese and British bikes to compete. Harley needed to build a better racer in order to keep up. In 1972, the company built a new version of the XR750. But during the rest of the 1970s, Japanese-made two-stroke machines took all the racing honors.

Today, the best known Harley-Davidson **café racer** is the XLCR. (The café racer started in England, where motorcyclists raced between cafés.) The Harley café racer is often called "Big Black," or "Black Brute." The XLCR may not be the fastest bike, but it has that special Harley feel: raw, gutsy, and plain.

Chapter 8

Looking Ahead

More than 100,000 visitors came to Milwaukee to celebrate Harley-Davidson's 90th birthday party in 1993. Sixty thousand riders formed a mass parade from the Kenosha Airport into the city. A whole new crowd of fans enjoyed the spectacle of Harley roadracing.

Going Slow and Going Safe

A writer for *Cycle World* magazine tried to figure out why so many people go crazy over Harleys. He found out that "It's because Harleys are so good at going slow," as one

rider told him. "It's okay to go slow on a
Harley."

You may or may not agree, but you have to
admit that Harleys are powerful at any speed.
And not only are they sure and strong, they are
also safer than many other bikes.

Safety is built into every Harley, starting at
the early stages. The company's designers use
computers to spot weak points in a frame. In
the factory, workers test safety at every stage
of assembly.

The Legend Continues

Soon the Harley will be roaring into its second century. After 100 years of motorcycling, will people still thrill to the thunder of a Harley? Will they still work and tinker and sweat over this magnificent two-wheeled machine?

The answer might be found at Sturgis, South Dakota, during a week in early August. More than 100,000 riders will probably agree: the Harley-Davidson will be taking to the road for a long time to come.

Glossary

chain drive–a drive system made up of a series of connected links

configurations–the arrangement of motorcycle parts on a frame

cylinder–the container for an engine piston as it moves up and down

cubic centimeter–the area covered by the stroke of the piston (also used to measure the size of the cylinder)

customize–to change a factory-built bike according to your own tastes

drive belt–a durable rubber belt sometimes used on motorcycles in place of a metal link chain

engine head–a flat cast iron or aluminum part that rests on top of the engine cylinder

Evolution engine–an engine developed in the 1980s that built on previous engine designs. Also called the Blockhead engine.

incorporated–to be legally set up as a business

intake valves–used to carry fuel and air into an engine

rebel–to oppose an established authority

torque–a twisting force that can be changed into motion

V-Twin–a design that places two cylinders at a 45-degree angle, giving the engine a distinctive sound

vandals–persons who willfully destroy property

To Learn More

Bygrave, Mike and Jim Dowdall. *Motor Cycle.*
New York: Gloucester Press, 1978.

Girdler, Allan. *Harley-Davidson: The
American Motorcycle.* Osceola, WI:
Motorbooks International, 1992.

Kahaner, Ellen. *Motorcycles.* Mankato, MN:
Capstone Press, 1991.

Norris, Martin. *Rolling Thunder.* Philadelphia:
Courage Books, 1992.

Taylor, Rich. *Street Bikes; A Golden Wheels
Book.* New York: Golden Press, 1975.

Wiesner, Wolfgang. *Harley-Davidson
Photographic History.* Osceola, WI:
Motorbooks International, 1989.

Index

47

Photo Credits:

Paul Dix: pp. 4, 6, 9, 10, 20, 23, 26, 28; *Big Twin*
magazine: pp. 12, 13, 14, 15, 16-17, 18, 25, 32, 34-35,
38, 40-41, 42; Harley-Davidson, p. 24.